TURKEY

WORLD ADVENTURES

BY STEFFI CAVELL-CLARKE

BookLife

BookLife
PUBLISHING

©2018
**BookLife Publishing
King's Lynn
Norfolk PE30 4LS**

All rights reserved.
Printed in Malaysia.

A catalogue record for this
book is available from the
British Library.

ISBN: 978-1-78637-512-4

Written by:
Steffi Cavell-Clarke

Edited by:
Robin Twiddy

Designed by:
Amy Li

*All facts, statistics, web addresses and URLs in this book were verified as valid and accurate at time of writing.
No responsibility for any changes to external websites or references can be accepted by either the author or publisher.*

TURKEY
WORLD ADVENTURES

CONTENTS

Words that look like **this** can be found in the glossary on page 24.

WHERE IS TURKEY?

Turkey is a country that sits on two **continents** called Asia and Europe. It is surrounded by both land and sea.

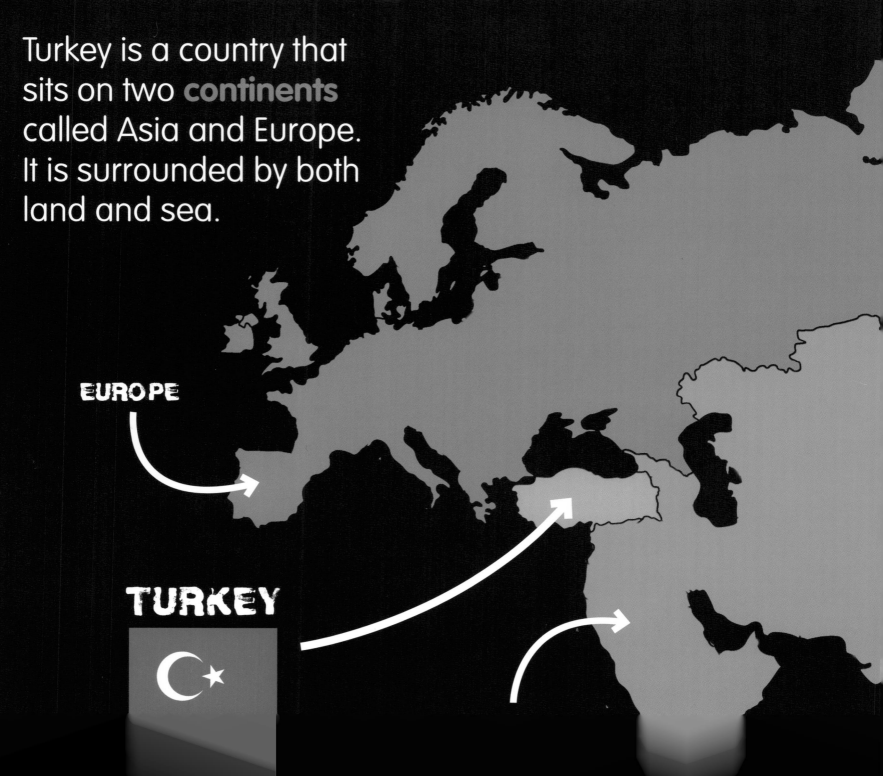

EUROPE

TURKEY

ANKARA, TURKEY

The capital of Turkey is Ankara.

The **population** of Turkey is over eight million.
Many people live in large cities, such as Istanbul.

WEATHER AND LANDSCAPE

The **climate** changes across the country, but it is usually cooler near the **coast**. Many **tourists** visit Turkey in the summer to enjoy the hot weather.

Turkey has many different landscapes. It has very long coastlines, large lakes, high mountain peaks and flat, grassy **plains**.

LAKE VAN, TURKEY

Lake Van is the largest lake in the country.

CLOTHING

Şalvar (say: shal-var) are **traditional** baggy trousers made of soft fabric. They are still worn in Turkey today.

ŞALVAR

In the cities, people often wear modern clothing. People will wear loose, comfortable dresses or shorts in summer to keep cool.

RELIGION

THE SULTAN AHMED MOSQUE, ISTANBUL

The religion with the most followers in Turkey is Islam. People who follow Islam are called Muslims. Their place of **worship** is called a mosque.

Everyone must wash their hands and feet before entering a mosque. This is a sign of respect to Allah.

FOOD

SKEWER

The kebab is one of Turkey's most popular dishes. Meat is placed onto a skewer and is grilled over a hot charcoal fire. Traditionally, the meat is either lamb or beef.

Baklava is a famous Turkish dessert. It is made from layers of pastry with chopped nuts and held together with syrup or honey.

AT SCHOOL

Children in Turkey go to school from the age of 6 until they are 18. They study Turkish, geography, maths, and science.

The main languages spoken in Turkey are Turkish and Kurdish.

Turkish children also have to study a **foreign** language. The most common language to study is English, but they can also study German, French or Spanish.

AT HOME

Turkish families can be very large and they often live together. Many families live in flats in large cities, such as Istanbul.

FLATS IN ISTANBUL

There are also lots of people who live in small villages and towns, where there are many fields to farm.

FAMILIES

Many children in Turkey live with their parents and brothers and sisters at home. They may also live with other family members, such as their grandparents.

HUMMUS

FALAFEL

TABBOULEH

Turkish families like to get together to celebrate special occasions such as religious festivals and birthdays. They often celebrate by eating special food and singing songs.

SPORT

Football is the most popular sport in Turkey. Many fans go and watch football to support their favourite team.

Other popular sports in Turkey include volleyball and basketball. Many children learn how to play sports, such as football, at school.

FUN FACTS

EPHESUS, TURKEY

Over seven million tourists visit Turkey every year. They go to see the amazing natural landscapes and **historic** sites, like the ancient Greek city of Ephesus.

Turkish **folklore** is full of magical creatures such as dragons, elves, wizards and genies. There are hundreds of fairy tales that are still told to children today.

23

GLOSSARY

climate	the common weather in a certain place
coast	land that meets the sea
continents	Earth's main areas of land
folklore	traditional beliefs or stories
foreign	another country or language
historic	famous or important in history
plains	large areas of flat land
population	number of people living in a place
tourists	people who visit another place for pleasure
traditional	ways of behaving that have been done for a long time
worship	a religious act such as praying

INDEX